HOW DO I DO IT?

Grayscale coloring is super easy! Simply pick out the colors you want to use, and start coloring. Color lightly over the image, and the shading underneath shows through giving the image depth and dimension.

This technique works best with colored pencils. Layer each color a little at a time. Pushing too hard and adding too dark of a color at one time can cover the shading underneath.

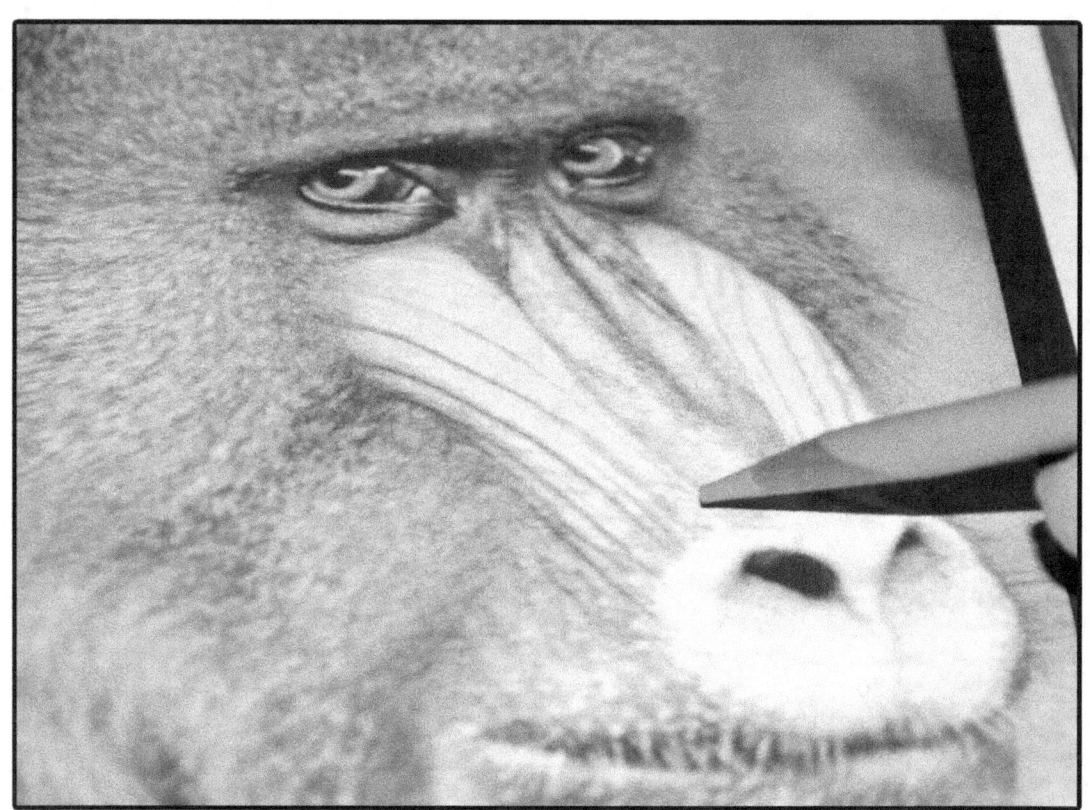

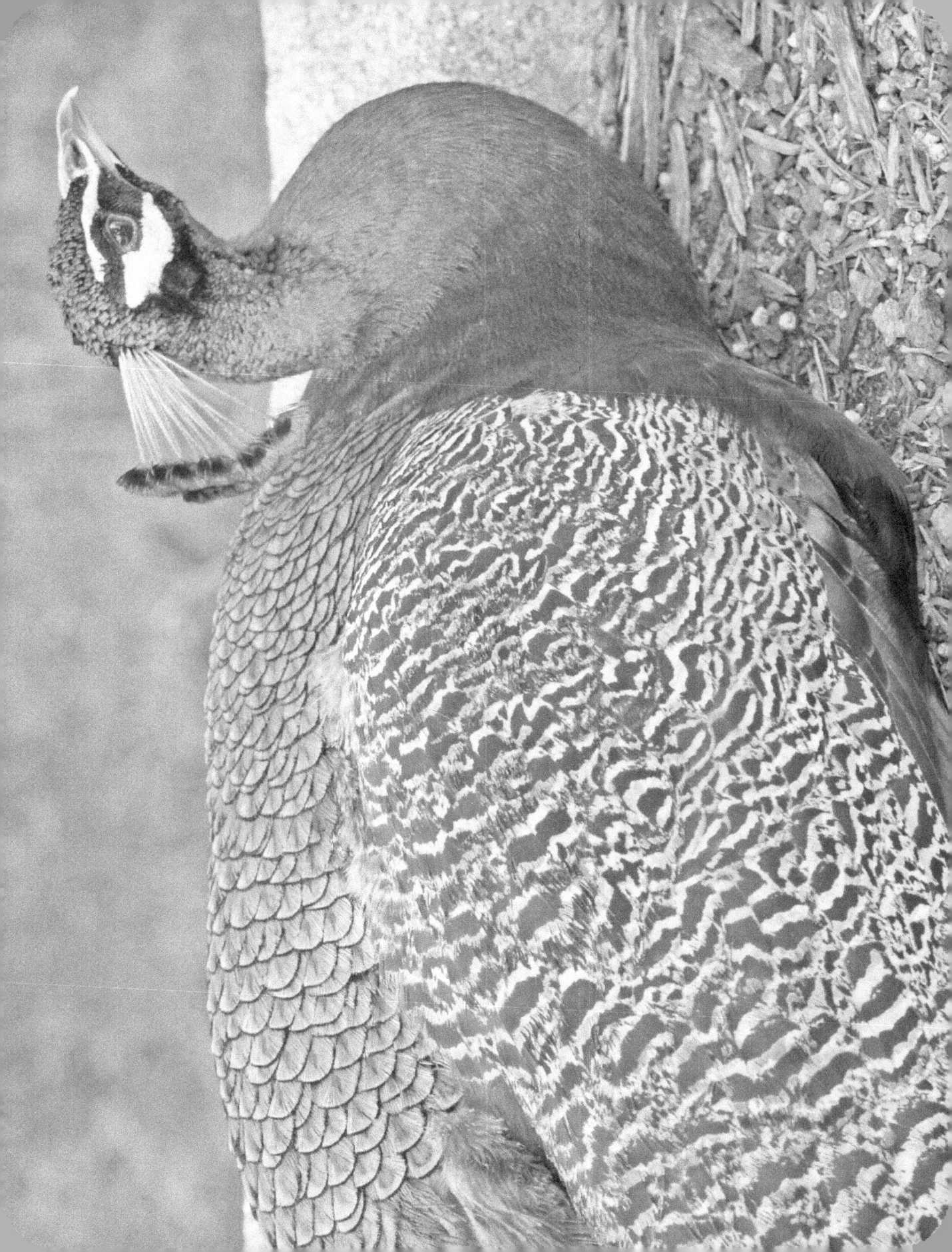

www.ingramcontent.com/pod-product-compliance
Lightning Source LLC
Chambersburg PA
CBHW080831310526
45788CB00019B/3125